THAT GETS YOU
INTERVIEWED!

To Deirdre

Áine Keenan is founder of *The Career Doctor* in Dublin,
providing career analysis and planning, training in job
targeting, CV preparation and interview skills. She has
extensive experience in careers counselling, and
preparation for return to work, career change or career
improvement. Having previously worked in the fields of
education, accountancy and banking, she has direct
experience of the real needs of employers in a modern and
rapidly changing workplace.

THE NEW
C.V.
THAT GETS YOU
INTERVIEWED!

ÁINE KEENAN

WOLFHOUND PRESS

First published 1994 by
WOLFHOUND PRESS Ltd
68 Mountjoy Square
Dublin 1

© 1994 Áine Keenan

All rights reserved. No part of this book may be reproduced or utilised in any form or by any means electronic or mechanical including photocopying, filming, recording, video recording, photography, or by any information storage and retrieval system, or shall not by way of trade or otherwise, be lent, resold or otherwise circulated in any form of binding or cover other than that in which it is published without prior permission in writing from the publisher. The moral rights of the author have been asserted.

British Library Cataloguing-in-Publication Data
    Keenan, Aine
    New CV That Gets You Interviewed
    I. Title
    650.14

    ISBN 0 86327 424 2

Cover design: Joe Gervin
Typesetting: Wolfhound Press
Printed by the Guernsey Press Co Ltd, Guernsey, Channel Isles

CONTENTS

THE CV PROCESS

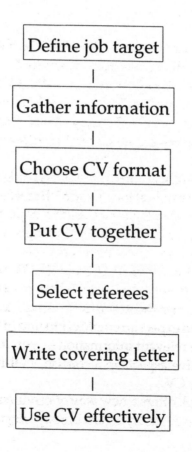

Define job target

|

Gather information

|

Choose CV format

|

Put CV together

|

Select referees

|

Write covering letter

|

Use CV effectively

INTRODUCTION

How successful would your CV be if it was one of a bundle of 500 from which twelve candidates were to be called for interview? Would it be easy to read, follow and remember? Would it communicate your most relevant achievements and qualifications? Would it motivate a potential employer to want to meet you?

The traditional format of CV has failed miserably to meet the needs of the modern job market. Including everything about yourself in the hope that if your experience or qualifications don't get you the job, something else on the document will, is a complete waste of time, energy and money. Moreover, your most significant achievements are hidden amidst a mass of information. It is not enough to put everything in and expect an employer to find his or her own way to the relevant information — you must present your positive aspects in a concise, well-focused and persuasive CV.

This book offers a new way of producing a vibrant and effective CV. By following my suggestions, you will greatly increase the chances of your application being read by potential employers and, provided that your experience and qualifications are reasonably suited to the position on offer, you are likely to be called to put your case in person — at interview.

This new approach requires your active participation, and can take up to ten hours to complete. The rewards, however, are great. Not alone can you anticipate a significant increase in interviews but, in the process, can find a job which reflects your skills, lifestyle, interests and needs.

The sample CVs included in this book are an amalgam of the most successful ones I have prepared for clients. Details have been edited to retain confidentiality, but this does not in any way alter their effectiveness. Use them as a guide to design a document that encourages employers to want to meet *you*. After all, that's what your CV is all about.

Chapter One

DEFINING YOUR JOB TARGET

When I prepare CVs on behalf of clients, my first question often surprises them: what position are you targeting? Some have responded with a blank stare and have attempted to deflect my query by mumbling something vague about 'waiting until the CV is ready before deciding' or 'not needing to make a definite choice just yet'. Others, being more adept at handling apparently inane questions, have announced that they'll 'take anything that's going' or that they 'simply want a general CV to reply to advertisements in the newspapers'. A small minority, however, have replied with confidence, detailing those jobs and careers which they have identified as reflecting their skills, interests and work values. These are people who have saved themselves considerable time and effort by approaching the CV preparation process with clarity and direction.

What is a Job Target?

A job target is a clear description of a specific occupation or career which you are willing to pursue with enthusiasm. Some examples of job targets include mechanical engineer, secretary, electrician, public relations executive and estate agent. Since the skills and abilities needed for many jobs are broadly similar, you will probably identify a number of job targets which interest you. If you work out in advance which jobs and careers you wish to target, you will be able to prepare an effective CV — one that communicates your most relevant achievements and highlights your future potential to encourage each targeted employer to call you for interview.

This chapter identifies job targets based on your skills, interests and values. If you already have job targets in mind, use this process to see how they measure up to your findings about yourself. Are you really suited to the job you have in mind? Is that really what you want to do?

Self-Assessment

Self-assessment means identifying your skills, detailing your interests and defining your values. Only by having a sharp focus on who you are and what you want will you be able to consider properly the options available to you.

Identifying your Skills

Your skills are the abilities you possess which will produce specific measurable results for an employer. Most of us take for granted the range of abilities we use every day in our work and so fail to realise what exactly we have to contribute. You must assess your range of marketable skills if you are to sell your unique potential in your CV.

Read over the following list of marketable skills and rate yourself on each as follows:

Very competent	4
Can do this well	3
Can manage this task	2
Not good at	1
Never tested	X

What I can do well . . .

— Teaching, training, helping people to learn
— Showing understanding and intuition for others
— Persuading, negotiating or selling a product or idea
— Giving useful help and support to people in need
— Designing events or learning activities
— Writing clearly, creatively and effectively
— Interpreting financial and statistical reports

— Working creatively with music
— Developing, adapting and extending other people's ideas
— Discovering why things are not working properly
— Memorising, retaining and learning information
— Fashioning and shaping objects or materials
— Working creatively with colours
— Gathering and researching information methodically
— Following instructions, plans or diagrams
— Working skilfully with your hands
— Providing alternative strategies to solve problems
— Possessing good hand-to-eye co-ordination
— Building, constructing or making things
— Encouraging people to talk about themselves
— Analysing, classifying and organising information
— Repairing and fixing things
— Identifying inconsistencies in ideas and opinions
— Anticipating, discovering and diagnosing problems
— Sorting through objects with precision and speed
— Extracting essential information from written documents
— Using hand tools and power tools
— Creating innovative and alternative ideas easily
— Expressing feelings and thoughts by painting
— Understanding and finding out how things work

— Manipulating, calculating and computing numbers quickly
— Working creatively with faces, shapes and patterns
— Budgeting, managing money and keeping accounts
— Expressing feelings through body, face and voice
— Counting and classifying stock
— Speaking effectively in a group or in public

Review those skills for which you have rated yourself as being very competent (i.e. those with a score of 4). Identify the five in which you are most qualified. Finally, list these marketable skills below in order of their satisfaction for you.

Summary of Skills

1. _____

2. _____

3. _____

4. _____

5. _____

Detailing your Interests

Your interests are the activities you prefer to perform at work. Go through the workplace activities listed below and rate your preference for each as follows:

Love doing	4
Quite enjoy	3
Tolerate	2
Dislike	1

What I enjoy doing . . .

— Writing reports, proposals or letters
— Persuading and motivating individuals or groups
— Operating machinery or equipment
— Counselling or advising others
— Maintaining financial and non-financial records
— Training or teaching people
— Interpreting documents and reports
— Working outdoors with plants or animals
— Negotiating between individuals and groups
— Interviewing people
— Helping others to find or retrieve information
— Manufacturing or producing goods
— Taking care of children or elderly people
— Investigating or researching information
— Working creatively with music, art or dance

— Organising projects, people and ideas
— Typing and doing desktop publishing with computers
— Painting, restoring or repairing things
— Working with accounts, budgets or statistical information
— Following written instructions from plans or blueprints
— Making presentations to groups
— Evaluating ideas
— Working with colours, shapes or materials

Go back over those interests which you love to do (i.e. those with a score of 4). Identify those five which you most enjoy, and list them in order of satisfaction they would bring you if incorporated into your job.

Summary of Interests

1. _____

2. _____

3. _____

4. _____

5. _____

Defining your Values

Your values reflect the importance of different aspects of the environment in which you work. Read down the list of work values below and rate yourself on each:

Vital	4
Very Important	3
Important	2
Doesn't matter	1

What matters to me . . .

— Having a safe job with regular income
— Being in a respected position
— Working on a variety of tasks and assignments
— Making decisions about how and when my work is done
— Having a good chance of promotion
— Doing something which is physically demanding
— Being able to help individuals or groups
— Working to deadlines
— Expressing ideas in writing, music or art
— Meeting new people or extending my social life
— Learning new things
— Being of service to the community
— Experiencing excitement often
— Working in a team with others
— Earning a good salary

— Having flexible working hours
— Making strong friendships with those at work
— Being in a position to take risks
— Working at tasks which require concentration
— Having authority over others
— Working near home
— Being an expert or specialist
— Facing new problems and challenges regularly
— Having a steady, planned work routine
— Working alone
— Working in a clean or modern environment
— Having the opportunity to travel

Review the values you have rated as being vital (i.e. those with a score of 4). Identify the five needs you consider to be most important, and list them below.

Summary of Values

1. _____

2. _____

3. _____

4. _____

5. _____

SELECTING YOUR JOB TARGET

Now that you know your key skills, interests and values, you should be much clearer about the range of jobs you would enjoy, and that reflect your personality.

If you already have job targets in mind, see how they measure up to your findings about yourself. If not, use your lists of skills, values and interests to identify ten job targets. To broaden the net, you might even ask a friend to read your lists of skills, interests and values, and to identify a job for the person they describe. Use your imagination. Identify jobs for which you are suited, regardless of the likelihood of actually finding work in a given area.

Potential Job Targets

1. _____

2. _____

3. _____

4. _____

5. _____

6. _____

7. _____

8. _____

9. _____

10. _____

Running out of ideas? The following list of 100 job targets is taken from employment advertisements in national and local newspapers. Try going through the list and identifying jobs that might be of interest to you.

Accountant
Fund raiser
Travel agency clerk
Wardrobe assistant
Prison officer
Market researcher
Secretary
Chef
Computer programmer
Public relations officer
Librarian
Sales assistant
Systems analyst
Cashier
Hairdresser
Tourist information officer
Doctor
Tax adviser
Solicitor
Proof-reader
Building society clerk
Designer
Driving instructor
Environmental health officer
Counsellor
Detective
Astrologer
Day care centre worker

Translator
Speech therapist
Laboratory technician
Clerical officer
Beauty therapist
Researcher (Radio/
television)
Veterinary surgeon
Journalist
Antique furniture
restorer
Reflexologist
Town planner
Illustrator
Investment analyst
Probation officer
Teacher
Nurse
Financial adviser
Author
Osteopath
Make-up artist
Quality control inspector
Hotel receptionist
Painter
Biochemist
Airline counter clerk
Engineer
Customs officer
Self-defence teacher
Estimator

Chemist
Plumber
Upholsterer
Horticulturist
Product manager
Quantity surveyor
Print worker
Carpenter
Traffic warden
Advertising executive
Estate agent
Buyer
Image consultant
Air Hostess/ Steward
Drama teacher
Midwife
Psychologist
Dentist
Garda
Dietician
Electrician
Interior designer
Composer
Social worker
Machinist
Trade union official
Office manager
Economist
Photographer
Graphic designer
Bus/train driver

Property manager   Caterer
Bar worker   Actor
Sales representative Actuary
Lecturer   Montessori teacher
Dressmaker   Waiter/Waitress
Aerobics teacher
Bookkeeper

Finally, reduce your list to three job targets for which you consider yourself best suited. Rank these in order of preference.

Selected Job Targets

1. _____

2. _____

3. _____

Now that you know what you are aiming for, it will be much easier for you to prepare an effective CV which reflects your personal objectives and abilities, as well as stimulating interest and enthusiasm among those who read it.

Chapter Two

GATHERING YOUR INFORMATION

The purpose of your CV is to highlight those aspects of your education and experience which are most useful to the job you have targeted. To pinpoint these, you must make a detailed analysis of your background to date. When you have done this you will probably have more information than you or your potential employer is interested in knowing, but you will then be able to go back over the outline, revise it, cut out words and information that will not be missed and rewrite paragraphs more concisely.

Begin by identifying the selling points which will differentiate your CV from those of other candidates applying for the same job — your achievements. Remember, these will be the cornerstones on which your CV is built.

Achievements

Your achievements are things you have done personally which have solved a problem, improved circumstances or made a contribution to a particular activity
or job. They provide hard evidence that you have
performed well for others and are therefore likely to
do the same again for any future employer.

Some examples of achievements include:
- Developed fluency in French and Spanish.
- Co-ordinated and directed an advertising
  campaign.
- Managed local Gaelic football team.
- Prepared written material for publication.
- Examined client's financial records and reports.
- Increased sales and profits.
- Reduced absenteeism.
- Investigated customer complaints.
- Provided facts and statistics for reports.
- Launched an in-house newsletter.
- Organised press conferences.
- Employed and trained new staff.

Where possible, you should assign quantities or values to your achievements to enhance the description
of what you have done.

For example:
- Designed proposal and secured government
  grant of £10,000.

- Increased sales of cars by 20% over a 3-month period.
- Reduced absenteeism by 15%, saving the company £25,000 in the first year.

Go through the following list of action verbs and place a tick beside any which may help to describe a personal, voluntary or work-related achievement.

Achieved	Contacted	Eliminated
Acquired	Contracted	Employed
Addressed	Converted	Encouraged
Administered	Co-ordinated	Established
Advertised	Corresponded	Evaluated
Advised	Counselled	Examined
Analysed	Created	Expanded
Appointed	Decreased	Exposed
Approved	Defined	Extracted
Arbitrated	Delivered	Facilitated
Arranged	Demonstrated	Forecasted
Assembled	Designed	Formulated
Assessed	Detected	Generated
Audited	Developed	Guided
Bought	Devised	Handled
Built	Diagnosed	Identified
Calculated	Directed	Implemented
Changed	Discovered	Improved
Collected	Distributed	Increased
Completed	Documented	Informed
Conducted	Drafted	Initiated
Consulted	Edited	Inspected

Installed   Organised   Reviewed
Instituted   Performed   Selected
Instructed   Planned   Served
Interpreted   Prepared   Sold
Interviewed   Produced   Stimulated
Introduced   Programmed   Strengthened
Investigated   Provided   Studied
Judged   Published   Supervised
Launched   Purchased   Supplied
Led   Recommended   Supported
Lectured   Recorded   Surveyed
Located   Recruited   Tested
Maintained   Reduced   Trained
Managed   Reorganised   Translated
Marketed   Replaced   Upgraded
Monitored   Represented   Used
Negotiated   Researched   Wrote
Observed   Resolved
Operated   Restored

Now, taking each action verb you have ticked,
write a sentence which describes your achievement
and creates the maximum impact with the minimum
words. Don't stop until you have at least twenty
achievements listed.

List of Achievements

1. _____
_____

2. _____
_____

3. _____
_____

4. _____
_____

5. _____
_____

6. _____
_____

7. _____
_____

8. _____
_____

9. _____
_____

10. _____
_____

11. _____

_____

12. _____

_____

13. _____

_____

14. _____

_____

15. _____

_____

16. _____

_____

17. _____

_____

18. _____

_____

19. _____

_____

20. _____

_____.

THE CV OUTLINE

You are now ready to assemble a draft outline of your work experience and educational background. Fill out the following form as comprehensively as possible. Remember, although not all of it may be required in your CV, it will be very useful if you are asked to fill out an application form.

EDUCATION AND TRAINING

Second Level

School   Dates Attended
_____

Intermediate/Junior Certificate Results
_____

_____

_____

Leaving Certificate Results
_____

_____

_____

Other Achievements
_____

_____

_____

Third Level

College _____

Dates Attended _____ Graduated _____

Degree/Diploma _____

Grade _____

Subjects Studied _____

_____

_____

_____

_____

College _____

Dates Attended _____ Graduated _____

Degree/Diploma _____

Grade _____

Subjects Studied _____

_____

_____

_____

_____

Vocational Training

Course   Dates Attended
_____

Certificate
_____

Skills Learned
_____

_____

_____

_____

Course   Dates Attended
_____

Certificate
_____

Skills Learned
_____

_____

_____

_____

Course   Dates Attended
_____

Certificate
_____

Skills Learned
_____

_____

_____

_____

SPECIAL SKILLS

Languages (Degree of Fluency)

_____

_____

_____

_____

_____

OTHER SKILLS

Typing, Wordprocessing, Writing, etc.

_____

_____

_____

_____

_____

_____

_____

_____

WORK EXPERIENCE

From   To
_____

Employer
_____

Address
_____

_____

Position and Title
_____

Achievements (Refer to pages 26/27 and indicate

appropriate numbers)
_____

_____

_____

From   To
_____

Employer
_____

Address
_____

_____

Position and Title
_____

Achievements (Refer to pages 26/27 and indicate

appropriate numbers)
_____

_____

_____

From _____ To _____

Employer _____

Address _____

_____

Position and Title _____

Achievements (Refer to pages 26/27 and indicate

appropriate numbers) _____

_____

_____

OTHER ACHIEVEMENTS AND EXPERIENCE

Voluntary Work _____

_____

_____

Sporting _____

_____

_____

_____

Other _____

_____

_____

_____

PROFESSIONAL AFFILIATIONS

_____

_____

_____

_____

_____

Congratulations. You have now collected the basic information for your CV. Before you move on, however, take this opportunity to go back and read over all of the sections again to see if you can improve on what you have already included.

Confident that you have gathered all relevant information, you are now ready to choose the best kind of CV for your specific needs.

Chapter Three

CHOOSING A CV
FORMAT

Most of us are unaware that there are many different formats of CV to choose from. We learn the traditional layout at secondary school which, while definitely detailed and biographical, fails miserably to highlight the best aspects of our education and experience. Most of my own clients were interested when I showed them some alternative formats, and were totally won over by the increase in interviews to which they were subsequently invited. Use this chapter to choose a format of CV which will reach out on your behalf to an employer and say: 'I am the person you're looking for'.

I am convinced that there are really only three effective CV formats you need to know. By effective, I mean that will get you an interview. Which format you use depends largely on your background and your future job target.

1. Chronological Format

This format lists your work experience by date, with the most recent job first and the others appearing in reverse chronological order. Each job listing shows your employer's name and location, dates of employment, job title and main achievements, with the most space being devoted to recent employment.

Advantages:
- Easy to prepare and follow.
- Most familiar format for Irish employers.
- Highlights growth and development in responsibility.
- Demonstrates stability if you have been with one employer for a long time.
- Emphasises the name of a prestigious employer and job title.

Disadvantages:
- Stresses gaps in your employment.
- Highlights age.
- Emphasises lack of experience.
- Raises questions if you have changed jobs frequently.
- Focuses on your most recent job, even if this was not your most important.

SEAN BRENNAN
25 Carysfort Road
Blackrock
Co. Dublin
(01) 2872349

WORK EXPERIENCE:

1990 - Present   **XPRESS OFFICE SUPPLIES LTD**   Dublin
Regional Sales Manager

- Employed and trained a new sales team of 10 which increased sales by 15% and profit margins by 10% in their first year.

- Co-ordinated trade show which attracted additional orders of £35,000.

- Negotiated new distributors in the Kildare area, resulting in an £85,000 increase in sales within 18 months.

- Designed a marketing plan which captured 55% of the Dublin market in 2 years.

1986 - 1990   **IRISH COMPUTERS LTD**   Cork
Sales Representative

- Sold £420,000 worth of personal computers over 6 months to small, medium and large buyers, with a profit margin of 25%.

- Awarded Salesperson of the Year 1987, 1989, 1990

- Exceeded sales targets by on average 30% in Cork/Kerry area for 4 years consecutively.

- Generated 24 new accounts and brought back 10 lost accounts.

EDUCATION:

1986   **MARKETING INSTITUTE OF IRELAND**
Diploma in Marketing

1984   **REGIONAL TECHNICAL COLLEGE, CORK**
Degree in Business Studies (Honours)

LANGUAGES:

1985   **ROYAL SOCIETY OF ARTS**
French for Commercial Purposes Stage III

1984   **INSTITUTE OF LINGUISTS**
Advanced Certificate in French

2. Functional Format

This format arranges your work experience according to functions or major areas of involvement. The order depends on your future job target. No attention is paid to the chronology of events: instead your major areas of achievement are emphasised. Dates, job titles and employer details are not highlighted.

Advantages:
- Captures the interest of the reader instantly.
- Focuses on achievements rather than lack of experience.
- Eliminates repetition of responsibilities.
- De-emphasises your most recent position if it is inferior to your earlier jobs.
- Highlights the scope of your experience.
- Presents achievements or experience gained outside of regular employment — voluntary, sporting, travel, social or other areas.

Disadvantages:
- More difficult format to prepare.
- Unpopular for traditional fields such as teaching, nursing, etc. where previous employers are of particular interest.
- Arouses confusion if not correctly targeted at a specific employer.
- Requires several worthwhile achievements.
- Avoids demonstrating stability or career growth.

EILIS MURPHY
16 St. Anne's Park
Tuam
Co. Galway
(091) 674362

TELEVISION
- Directed *The Way We Were*, a 10 part documentary on the changing face of Irish society, an RTE and Channel 4 co-production.
- Produced 60 episodes of *Blarney*, Ireland's most popular soap ever, topping TAM ratings for 3 consecutive years.
- Edited *Green, Black and Blue*, a series of short films on the subject of modern art in Ireland.

RADIO
- Produced *Siopa*, a 1-hour play for Radio 1, winner of John Player Drama Awards, 1992.
- Broadcast 15 reports, each of 30 minutes duration, on successful community initiatives in the west of Ireland.

JOURNALISM
- Wrote over 150 articles on fashion, make-up and beauty care for the *Connacht Tribune, City Tribune* and *The Sentinel*.
- Edited *Inside Business*, the Chamber of Commerce of Ireland bi-monthly publication, with a 10,000 copy nationwide circulation.
- Contributed articles on a freelance basis to *The Irish Independent, Evening Herald* and *Phoenix Magazine*.

EMPLOYMENT HISTORY:

1988 - Present	RTE, Dublin Director/Producer
1987 - 1988	Diflin Publications, Dublin Editor
1985 - 1987	Connacht Tribune Newspapers, Galway Fashion Editor

EDUCATION:

1985	College of Commerce, Rathmines Certificate in Journalism, 10 Honours
1983	University College Galway B.Comm. (2.1 Honours)

3. Targeted Format

The targeted format lists those tasks you are able to do (abilities) and those you have actually done in the past (achievements) which are specifically related to the position you are targeting. The emphasis at all times is on identifying the needs of a potential employer and producing evidence to prove you can match those needs.

Advantages:
- Easy format to prepare.
- Emphasises future potential rather than lack of past experience.
- Communicates clearly to the reader that you have identified his or her needs.
- Avoids focusing on age.
- Makes an excellent case for one specific job.
- Demonstrates a willingness to do solid research on the employer.

Disadvantages:
- Unsuited to certain traditional occupations, eg. teaching.
- Requires considerable research on a range of employers.
- Arouses confusion if employer's needs are misinterpreted.
- Based on the assumption that you are sure of your job target.
- Needs a different CV for each application.

PATRICK RYAN
23 Main Street
Mallow
Co. Cork
(021) 316376

JOB TARGET: HOTEL DUTY MANAGER

ABILITIES:

- Perform all reception and front-office tasks including taking reservations, managing floats and handling queries and complaints.

- Produce end-of-day computerised reports, identifying and reconciling disclosed errors.

- Schedule, organise and manage functions, liaising between guests and staff.

- Oversee the provision of a high quality restaurant service.

- Deal professionally and calmly with all sorts of problems, facilitating the satisfaction of the parties involved.

ACHIEVEMENTS:

- Performed reception shift alone for 125-room hotel with 85% occupancy, handling walk-in, reserved, group and inter-hotel bookings.

- Operated Opus front-of-house computer system, producing all relevant daily reports.

- Participated in all sizes and types of functions, providing additional support and backup when needed.

- Provided à la carte and table d'hôte style service in a range of high quality establishments.

- Worked in hotel bars and nightclubs, both in a serving and cashiering capacity.

WORK EXPERIENCE:

May 1992 - to date	Jury's Hotel, Cork Assistant Duty Manager
April - Oct 1991	The Savoy, London Receptionist
Nov 1990 - Dec 1991	The Burlington Hotel, Dublin Banqueting Staff
June - Sept 1991	The Hilton, New York General Operations Staff

EDUCATION:

1992	TRINITY COLLEGE DUBLIN B.Sc. in Hotel and Catering Management (2:1 Honours)

Each of these formats keeps personal information to a minimum. This is in order to focus the reader's attention clearly on your achievements and potential. The traditional CV includes details such as where you were born, age, marital status, nationality and so on. These simply blur the picture and give the reader an opportunity for bias, or an excuse to eliminate you before the interview stage. By presenting this information in person at the interview itself, you can see and react to any difficulties the employer may have, rather than allowing yourself to be 'screened out' because of bias regarding age, social or economic factors.

Moreover, this type of CV fits onto a single page. Working to this rule will help you concentrate on minimising superfluous information and focus on the achievements which best support your cause.

Think carefully before you decide to let your CV run onto a second page. Is this absolutely necessary in order to express the wealth or diversity of your experience? Is all of the material included interesting and relevant enough to hold the attention of a busy reader? If you do feel that a one-page document is not enough to get you an interview, avoid using the second page as an excuse to let excessive phrases or unfocused information slip in. Balance your text evenly across the two pages. Do not add in extra text simply to fill the space.

Making a Decision

You should by now have an idea of which of the three formats you would like to follow. Remember, there is nothing to stop you from preparing more than one type of CV, depending on your own individual needs. However, if you are still unsure, here is an exercise which should help you decide.

Place a tick beside each statement which applies to you.

1. I am looking for my first full-time job. ❑ A
2. I would prefer to emphasise dates. ❑ B
3. I have held a wide variety of unconnected jobs in the past. ❑ A
4. I am willing to write an individual CV for each job target. ❑ C
5. I am returning to the job market after a considerable time. ❑ A
6. I only want to have to prepare one CV. ❑ B
7. I have considerable skills but little experience. ❑ C
8. I would like to emphasise the continuity of my employment record. ❑ B
9. I wish to change my career. ❑ A
10. I am very clear about the position I seek. ❑ C
11. I would like to highlight the names of my previous employers. ❑ B
12. I wish to make a very strong case for a specific job target. ❑ C

Check which letter you have ticked most frequently and identify the format of CV most suited to your needs.

> A = Functional Format;
> B = Chronological Format;
> C = Targeted Format.

The final choice is yours.

The format of CV I intend to follow is _____

Chapter Four

PUTTING YOUR CV TOGETHER

At last! I hear you say. Your investment is to be rewarded. You can now begin to put together a document which will stand out from the crowd and get you interviews.

Depending on which format you have chosen to follow, you can turn immediately to the relevant page and start right away.

Preparing a Chronological CV, page 46

Preparing a Functional CV, page 50

Preparing a Targeted CV, page 55

Preparing a Chronological CV

1. *The Heading*

Write your name, address and telephone number (with area code) centred at the top of a blank page. Put your name in capital letters, and the address in initial capital letters and lower case. I suggest that you use your home telephone number only, where possible, to avoid suspicions that your current employer may actually want you to get another job.

2. *Work Experience*

Under the heading *Work Experience*, and starting with your present or most recent position, transcribe the dates of employment, employer name and location, and job title (as assembled on pages 32/33).

- If you have had many employers, list only the last four or five, unless earlier positions are exceptionally relevant.
- Be consistent from one employer listing to the next.
- Put the employer name in capital letters.
- Avoid taking up space with a full employer address; the town or city will usually be sufficient.
- Use years, and not months, when detailing the dates of employment.

Beneath each employer listing, insert in bulleted form (eg. •) only those significant achievements (as assembled on pages 26/27) which are relevant to your job target.

Put your strongest statements at the top, and work your way downwards.

Keep your job target firmly in mind. The purpose of the exercise is to communicate to the potential employer that your past experiences clearly demonstrate your ability to perform your targeted job. With each insertion, ask yourself: 'Will this encourage the employer to want to meet me?' or 'Will this be a turn off?' Make your decision to include or omit the statement accordingly.

3. Education

Under the heading *Education*, transcribe the dates, names of institutions attended and the certificates, diplomas or degrees awarded (as assembled on pages 28-30).

If you have a third level qualification, you can omit information about second level education (unless impressive and relevant).

List the highest qualifications first, giving the full name of the institutions, but not their addresses.

4. Affiliations

If you have membership of any professional organisations which are relevant to your job target, eg. the Marketing Institute of Ireland, Irish Institute of Industrial Engineers or Institute of Taxation, then include them under the heading *Affiliations*.

5. *Corrections and Adjustments*

Read back over this first draft carefully. Make sure that you have not forgotten any relevant information or omitted any time periods. Check to ensure that the sentences and paragraphs are kept short and to the point. Eliminate all spelling mistakes, inaccuracies, repetition and irrelevant details. Finally, rewrite the draft outline as many times as it takes to satisfy yourself completely that this document represents the best that you have to offer and is capable of convincing a prospective employer that you have what he or she is looking for. When you have done this, turn to page 60 for instructions on the final typing and printing.

MARY RYAN
124 Ennis Road
Limerick
Co. Limerick
(061) 682357

WORK EXPERIENCE

IRISH CAR SUPPLIES LTD.   **1988 - Present**

Limerick

Warehouse Manager

- Supervised, co-ordinated and managed the activities of over 40 full-time and 20 part-time employees for a major distributor of car parts.

- Reorganised storage space over a 6-month period to accommodate a 35% increase in stocks.

- Designed a new checking system which reduced errors on delivery notes by 10% per annum.

- Developed training procedures and safety standards for both full-time and part-time staff in compliance with ISO 9000.

- Established incentive schemes for attendance which reduced absenteeism by 18% and saved the company £60,000 over 2 years.

CARGO EXPRESS LTD.   **1986 - 1988**

Nenagh

Warehouse Supervisor

- Supervised 10-15 full-time employees engaged in the loading and unloading of lorries and vans.

- Verified quantities, counted parts and filled orders.

- Designed a loading diagram which increased the space in lorries and vans by 10%.

- Reduced pilferage by £16,000 in 1988.

EDUCATION

DUBLIN CITY UNIVERSITY   **1986**

Degree in Business Studies (Distinction)

TRALEE RTC   **1984**

Diploma in Business Studies (Credit)

AFFILIATIONS
Institute of Irish Warehouse Managers

Preparing a Functional CV

1. *The Heading*
Write your name, address and telephone number (with area code) centred at the top of a blank page. Put your name in capital letters, and the address in initial capital letters and lower case. I suggest that you use your home telephone number only, where possible, to avoid suspicions that your current employer may actually want you to get another job.

2. *Work Experience*
Read through the following list of specific functions, and select those three or four which are most in line with your job target and best describe your particular areas of experience or expertise. Insert any additional functions you consider relevant to you personally at the end of the listing.

Accounting	Child Care
Acting	Coaching
Administration	Communications
Advertising	Computers
Agriculture	Consultancy
Architecture	Counselling
Art	Designing
Aviation	Dancing
Banking	Education
Beauty Therapy	Electronics
Catering	Engineering

Fashion
Film
Fishing
Forestry
Graphic Design
Hairdressing
Health Care
Horticulture
Insurance
Interior Design
Journalism
Law
Management
Marketing
Medicine
Mental Health
Modelling
Music
Navigation
Nursing
Nutrition
Office Work
Pharmaceuticals
Photography
Physiotherapy
Planning
Politics
Printing
Prison Service
Programming
Psychiatry

Psychology
Public Relations
Publishing
Radio
Sales
Secretarial
Security
Social Work
Systems Design
Taxation
Teaching
Television
Tourism
Travel
Typing
Word Processing
Writing
Youth Work

_____

_____

_____

_____

_____

_____

_____

_____

Start with the function heading most relevant to your job target, and work your way downwards in order of importance. Insert in bulleted form (eg. •) your most significant achievements (as assembled on pages 26/27) associated with each function you have selected. Remember, there is no particular need to identify which part of your employment record such achievements are related to.

The purpose of the exercise is to communicate to the potential employer that your past experiences clearly demonstrate your ability to perform your targeted job. With each insertion, ask yourself: 'Will this encourage the employer to want to meet me?' or 'Will this be a turn off?' Make your decision to include or omit the statement accordingly.

3. Employment Record

Under the heading *Experience* or *Employment Record*, and starting with your present or most recent position, transcribe the dates of employment, employer name and location, and job title (as assembled on pages 32/33).

- If you have had many employers, list only the last four or five, unless earlier positions are exceptionally relevant.
- Be consistent in listing your employers.
- Avoid taking up space with a full employer address; the town or city is usually sufficient.
- Use years, and not months, when detailing the dates of employment.

3. Education

Under the heading *Education*, transcribe the dates, names of institutions attended and your certificates, diplomas or degrees (as assembled on pages 28-30).

If you have a third level qualification, omit information about second level education (unless impressive and relevant).

List the highest qualifications first, giving the full name of the institutions, but not their addresses.

4. Affiliations

If you have membership of any professional organisations which are relevant to your job target, eg. the Marketing Institute of Ireland, Irish Institute of Industrial Engineers or Institute of Taxation, then include them under the heading *Affiliations*.

5. Corrections and Adjustments

Read back over this first draft carefully. Make sure that you have not forgotten any relevant information or omitted any time periods. Check to ensure that the sentences and paragraphs are kept short and to the point. Eliminate all spelling mistakes, inaccuracies, repetition and irrelevant details. Finally, rewrite the draft outline as many times as it takes to satisfy yourself completely that this document represents the best that you have to offer and is capable of convincing a prospective employer that you have what he or she is looking for. Then turn to page 60 for instructions on the final typing and printing.

FIONNUALA CLANCY
16 Sandycove Avenue
Dun Laoghaire
Co. Dublin
(01) 2835755

RECEPTION
- Maintained daily schedule of events and arranged meetings for 4 psychologists.
- Screened and directed phone calls, greeted visiting clients, sorted and directed post.
- Updated client records on arrival and departure from the clinic.
- Developed and maintained a computerised accounting system for the practice, increasing efficiency by 20%.

SECRETARIAL
- Typed reports, correspondence and labels on IBM and Apple Mac computers.
- Proficient on WordPerfect 6, Ami Pro 3.1, Word for Windows 6, Excel 2.0 and dBase IV.
- Established new manual filing system and co-ordinated new security system for minimising access to confidential information.
- Published and designed bi-monthly office newsletter.

CLERICAL
- Processed on average 200 invoices per week.
- Organised bank deposits, disbursing and balancing petty cash.
- Prepared and submitted monthly financial accounts.
- Reconciled bank statements with accounts, liaising with the bank to rectify discrepancies.

EMPLOYMENT RECORD:

1992 - Present	Creative Counselling, Bray Office Manager
1989 - 1992	3-D Films, Avoca Office Junior

EDUCATION:

1989	Senior College Dun Laoghaire Executive Secretarial Course
1988	Royal Society of Arts Certificate in Computer Literacy and Information Technology

Preparing a Targeted CV

1. The Heading
Write your name, address and telephone number (with area code) centred at the top of a blank page. Put your name in capital letters, and the address in initial capital letters and lower case. I suggest that you use your home telephone number only, where possible, to avoid suspicions that your current employer may actually want you to get another job.

2. Job Target
Beside the heading *Job Target*, insert in capital letters the description of the occupation or career which you are willing to pursue with enthusiasm.

3. Abilities
Under the heading *Abilities*, list in bulleted form (eg. •), six to eight statements outlining what you can do related to the job target you have specified above in a means which actively supports your application. Don't worry if you have not acquired the relevant experience yet. What is more important is to communicate the belief that you can perform these tasks. Remember, time spent on carefully researching the targeted employer's needs and matching them with your own abilities will compensate for any lack of experience.

4. Achievements

Using the heading *Achievements*, insert in bulleted form six to eight significant achievements (as assembled on pages 26/27) which will clearly demonstrate what you have done of relevance to your job target. Put your strongest statements at the top, and work your way downwards.

Keep your job target firmly in mind. The purpose of the exercise is to communicate to a potential employer that your achievements provide evidence to back up your claims about your abilities. With each insertion ask yourself: 'Will this encourage the employer to want to meet me?' or 'Will this be a turn off?' Make your decision to include or omit the statement accordingly.

5. Employment Record

Under the heading *Experience* or *Employment Record*, and starting with your present or most recent position, transcribe the dates of employment, employer name and location, and job title (as assembled on pages 32/33).

- If you have had many employers, list only the last four or five, unless earlier positions are exceptionally relevant.
- Be consistent from one employer listing to the next.
- Avoid taking up space with a full employer address; the town or city will usually be sufficient.

- Use years, and not months, when detailing the dates of employment.

6. *Education*

Under the heading *Education*, transcribe the dates, names of institutions attended and the certificates, diplomas or degrees awarded (as assembled on pages 28-30).

If you have a third level qualification, omit information about second level education (unless impressive and relevant).

List the highest qualifications first, giving the full name of the institutions, but not their addresses.

7. *Affiliations*

If you have membership of any professional organisations which are relevant to your job target, eg. the Marketing Institute of Ireland, Irish Institute of Industrial Engineers or Institute of Taxation, then include them under the heading *Affiliations*.

8. *Corrections and Adjustments*

Read back over this first draft carefully. Make sure that you have not forgotten any relevant information or omitted any time periods. Check to ensure that the sentences and paragraphs are kept short and to the point. Eliminate all spelling mistakes, inaccuracies, repetition and irrelevant details. Finally, rewrite the draft outline as many times as it takes to satisfy yourself completely that this document represents the best

that you have to offer and is capable of convincing a
prospective employer that you have what he or she is
looking for. When you have done this, turn to page 60
for instructions on the final typing and printing.

JOSEPH O'REILLY
Main Street
Letterkenny
Co. Donegal
(073) 662343

JOB TARGET: SECURITY GUARD

ABILITIES:

- Check credentials of persons and vehicles entering and leaving the premises.
- Carry out routine patrols on foot and by car.
- Monitor electronic security systems for intrusions.
- Verify that no unauthorised persons remain on the premises after working hours.
- Maintain radio contact with other security guards.
- Ensure that all alarms, fire extinguishers and electrical systems are working properly.

ACHIEVEMENTS:

- Carried out security operations on a 20-acre manufacturing site.
- Prevented a serious fire, which started in the warehouses, from spreading to the rest of the plant.
- Conducted investigations of internal and external theft, resulting in a 45% reduction of incidents.
- Developed a plan to reduce traffic in and out of the site, thereby resulting in improved warehouse security.
- Supervised a team of 2 security guards in the absence of the Security Manager.

EMPLOYMENT RECORD:

1990 - Present	Acorn Ltd., Buncrana Security Guard
1989 - 1990	Golden Dairies, Ballyshannon Security Guard
1988 - 1989	LCD Ltd, Downings Patrol Officer

EDUCATION:

1990	St. Eunan's College, Letterkenny Leaving Certificate — 3 Honours

Typing and Printing

Inputting

Once you have written the final draft of your CV, you need to type it up. Where possible, avoid using a typewriter, as a personal computer is much more flexible.

It will enable you to:
- create different versions and formats to satisfy your specific requirements;
- check for spelling, grammar and punctuation errors;
- adjust the material to stay within one page;
- retain copies which have gone to targeted employers;
- constantly update your most recent experience, and
- produce a professional looking document.

Do not despair, however, if you do not own this type of equipment. Use the services of a secretarial bureau specialising in inputting, laying out and printing high quality CVs. The better offices now use desktop publishing software and print documents on laser printers. Don't settle for anything less.

Laying Out

In order to highlight the most relevant parts and make your CV easy to read, there are a number of very useful techniques which you should follow:

- Use adequate margins (at least 1 inch wide) to create plenty of empty space on the page. This will make your CV easier to read.
- Organise information logically by indenting paragraphs.
- Leave adequate spacing between paragraphs.
- Use capital letters, bold or italics for emphasis. However, be consistent and don't overuse these techniques.
- Put bullets (eg. •) in front of each of the major achievements listed.

Proofing

Before the final printing of your CV, it is imperative that you present the document to at least three people you can trust to evaluate it critically. Get them to use the checklist on the next page as a guideline. Ask them to read the CV carefully for grammar, spelling and punctuation errors: it is better to get it right at this stage rather than when you have flawed copies in circulation! Finally, seek their opinions on how the document might be strengthened. Remember, however, that you must be the final judge of whether these ideas will bring about a more concise, well-focused and persuasive CV.

Printing

You are strongly advised to have all of your CVs

printed out on a laser printer. Photocopies are frequently smudged and of poor quality. Having come this far, now is not the time to skimp on expense. After all, it's your future you are investing in.

Always use 100 gram bond, A4 paper. The colour you choose is up to yourself. I suggest that you opt for ivory or buff paper. This will stand out from the sea of other CVs, letters and documents on an employer's desk.

You can rightly be proud of your finished CV and be confident that this powerful advertising tool will create a strong favourable impression on any prospective employer.

The best CV in the world, however, is not enough. It is how you use it that makes the difference: the following chapters will show you how to do just that.

CV CHECKLIST

- ☐ Fits onto one page
- ☐ One inch margins all round
- ☐ Adequate white space
- ☐ Good balance on the page
- ☐ High quality print
- ☐ 100 gram bond, A4 paper
- ☐ Name, address and telephone number centred at top of page
- ☐ Important points highlighted by capital letters, bold or italic type
- ☐ Bulleted lists of achievements and results
- ☐ Sentences and paragraphs short, sharp and clearly understood
- ☐ Strong action words used to stress achievements and results
- ☐ Amounts, percentages and figures included where possible
- ☐ Personal information omitted
- ☐ Misstatements or exaggerations avoided
- ☐ Spelling, grammar and punctuation errors eliminated

Chapter Five

SELECTING YOUR
REFEREES

It is amazing how many people put the names of referees on their CVs on the assumption that two or three individuals can recommend them for any position for which they apply. Remember, the purpose of your CV is to get you job interviews. It is only when you have done well in an interview that the names of referees are likely to be requested by a potential employer, to verify your credentials and provide more information where necessary. Likewise, until you have been interviewed and know what the potential employer is looking for, you will not know which referees to nominate.

If you circulate your CV to the recruitment agencies, be aware that there is every likelihood that the agency will phone any referees you name before they decide whether or not to send your details to potential employers. This could mean your referees are burdened with countless enquiries from people who are not even in a position to make you a job offer.

Therefore, unless specifically requested, the best option is not to nominate referees on your CV, but instead to include a statement to the effect that references are available on request.

The Referee Listing

It is essential that you have a list of referees with you when you appear for interview so that you can nominate those most appropriate, on request.

Try to have at least one referee for each position of employment you have identified on your CV. Where possible, you should also include people you know who work in the area you have targeted. For example, if you want to go into banking, a reference from a bank manager is better than one from a politician or a teacher. Those who will feel most comfortable discussing you and your work/achievements factually with any prospective employer are by far the best referees you can choose.

Once you identify a list of potential referees, your next step is to meet them personally and seek their permission and co-operation. Make sure that each of your referees is comfortable recommending you for the position(s) you are targeting. Give them a copy of the CV(s) that you are sending out, and try to review in advance what they are likely to say about you. Take the time to discuss those strong points about yourself which you consider could be of most benefit to you if made by your referee. Remember, however, that your referee may also be asked to describe your weaknesses, so make sure that you have discussed in detail what would be said in such circumstances. Finally, if you are nominating a former employer as a referee, make sure that you and your former employer have the circumstances of your departure worked out and agreed upon well in advance.

When you have met with all of the potential referees on your list and established those whom you feel confident will say the right things about you and avoid providing negative information of any sort, draw up your list of actual referees. Write to all those you have met, thanking them for their time. In the case of those you have decided to use on your referee listing, include a separate sheet outlining those strong points about yourself which you hope the referee will make if contacted by a potential employer.

Immediately after an interview, telephone the referees whose names you have given and alert them to expect a call. Brief them about the job, how your qualifications and experience fit it, and what your strong points are for the particular position. Request a copy of any written references sent for your files. By preparing carefully for all eventualities, you will have stacked the odds of success firmly in your favour.

Finally, when you get the job you are looking for, write thank-you letters to all your referees, letting them know of your new job and thanking them for

4. Name: _____

Title: _____

Company/organisation: _____

Address: _____

_____

Telephone: _____

5. Name: _____

Title: _____

Company/organisation: _____

Address: _____

_____

Telephone: _____

6. Name: _____

Title: _____

Company/organisation: _____

Address: _____

_____

Telephone: _____

Chapter Six

WRITING YOUR COVERING LETTER

The covering letter is used to accompany your CV when you are responding to an advertisement, writing to potential employers on speculation or following up a cold call in search of an interview. It allows you to personalise your CV and to tailor the information in it to the needs of a specific employer. Being the first document that the reader sees, it also sets the scene for the CV to follow. Your covering letter should answer the question: what can this person do that will be of value to the business? and should whet the reader's appetite for the CV.

1. The Addressee

If at all possible, address your letter to a specific individual. Make sure to verify the correct spelling of the name and title of the person to whom you are writing (by phoning the business, if necessary). Only use 'Dear Sir/Madam' if you are replying to a box number. Finally, unless you have no alternative, avoid addressing speculative letters to 'The Personnel Manager', as you will probably get a standard letter back (if you are lucky) thanking you for your enquiry, saying that they have nothing available at the moment and that they will keep your CV on file.

2. The Opening Paragraph

State the purpose of your letter immediately. This can be that you are responding to an advertisement, writing as a result of a suggestion of a mutual acquaintance, or forwarding your CV as a result of research which has motivated an interest in you to work for that particular employer. By including something in this paragraph which is unique to the person or business, you will show the reader that you have taken the time and effort to write a personal letter to him or her.

3. The Body of the Letter

In this section you highlight your marketable skills and achievements, and relate these to the needs of your potential employer. This active attempt to identify what you can contribute to the business involves considerable research, but it will impress the reader and increase your chances of gaining an interview.

If you are replying to an advertisement and your achievements, experience and education match the requirements exactly, organise your information in a way that highlights this.

This part of your application can also be treated as an opportunity to reflect some aspect of your personality. You might decide to mention relevant characteristics such as creativity, maturity, enthusiasm, etc.

4. The Closing Paragraph

Your closing statement asks for a meeting at the reader's earliest convenience, and/or states that you will take the next step by phoning within a specified period of time for an appointment.

COVERING LETTER CHECKLIST

☐ Fits onto one page
☐ One inch margins all round
☐ Good balance on the page
☐ High quality print (laser printed)
☐ 100 gram bond, A4 paper (same as CV)
☐ Addressed to a specific individual
☐ Focuses on potential employer's needs
☐ Matches these needs with significant achievements
☐ Misstatements or exaggerations avoided
☐ Arrangements for a meeting suggested
☐ Spelling, grammar and punctuation errors eliminated
☐ Signed personally

GENERAL LETTER IN RESPONSE TO AN ADVERTISEMENT

127 Main St
Ballina
Co. Mayo
(098) 317656

10th October, 1994

Ms Anne O'Keeffe
Personnel Manager
A.T. Cross & Co.
Ballinasloe
Co. Galway

Dear Ms O'Keeffe,

In response to the advertisement in the *Galway Advertiser*, 8th October, 1994, I am applying for the position as secretary.

During the past eight years, I have had a wide range of experience in all aspects of modern office practice, which included developing and maintaining a computerised accounting system. I am proficient on Word for Windows 2.0, Lotus 1-2-3 and dBase IV, type at 80 wpm and take shorthand at 120 wpm.

Please find enclosed a copy of my curriculum vitae for your consideration. I will be available for interview at your convenience and would welcome the opportunity to discuss both the position and my experience in greater detail. Looking forward to hearing from you.

Yours faithfully,

Maria Murphy

LETTER WITH CV IN RESPONSE TO AN ADVERTISEMENT

67 Ashe Street
Tralee
Co. Kerry
(066) 313664
16th March, 1995

Mr John O'Brien
Personnel Manager
Elida Gibbs (Irl.) Ltd.
20 Parkmore Industrial Estate
Dublin 8

Dear Mr O'Brien,

I am most interested in your advertisement for a Full-Time Trainer
and feel that my qualifications and experience meet your needs.

You Require	*My Experience*
Full-time Trainer, with Minimum 3 years General Teaching Experience	8 years full-time teaching Beauty Therapy
Organisation and Running of Courses	Set up, administered and ran courses including CIBTAC, CIDESCO, Electrolysis and Reflexology
Provision of Product Knowledge to Chemist's Assistants	3 years of experience dealing with a variety of product ranges
Life Science Graduate	B. Sc. (Hons.), UCD
Commercially Astute Candidate	Part-time Image Consultant

I would be most interested in discussing your needs personally,
and look forward to hearing from you.

Yours faithfully,

Eileen Lynch

LETTER FOLLOWING UP ON A 'COLD CALL'

8 Nth. Frederick St.
Dublin 1
(01) 6772151

30th August, 1994.

Mr Barry O'Kane
BOK Consultants
26 Northumberland Road
Ballsbridge
Dublin 4

Dear Mr O'Kane,

Thank you for taking my telephone call this morning. Our conversation increased my interest in your firm and confirmed that my skills and experience could be of value to you.

Enclosed is my curriculum vitae for your review and consideration. Although most of my work has been in the manufacturing industry, I am certain that my ability to identify complex and conflicting business problems and their root causes, to develop practical solutions and to secure consensus for their implementation could be of benefit to your firm.

I will call you later on this week, as you suggested, so that we can arrange a mutually convenient time for a meeting.

Yours faithfully,

Kevin McGuinness

LETTER USING A 'BRIDGE'

26 Main St.
Mullingar
Co. Westmeath
(0902) 553216

5th July, 1995

Mr Robert Dunne
Personnel Manager
McDonald's Restaurants
17 O'Connell St.
Dublin 1

Dear Mr Dunne,

Brendan Keane, your Chief Accountant, recently informed me of your plans to expand your chain of restaurants to Mullingar, and suggested that I contact you concerning the position of Restaurant Manager.

I have over fifteen years' experience in all areas of restaurant management, specialising for the last eight years in the establishment, supervision and management of fast food outlets on behalf of my current employer in Portlaoise, Tullamore, Ballinasloe and Nenagh. I am now seeking a new challenge and feel that I could be of value to your company in this your latest expansion.

Please find enclosed for your review and consideration my curriculum vitae. I will telephone you within the next three days to arrange an appointment and look forward to meeting you personally.

Yours faithfully,

Aidan Farrell

Chapter Seven

USING YOUR CV EFFECTIVELY

You want your new CV to generate as many interviews as you can, and from those interviews get firm job offers. The best CV in the world is ineffective unless you can find ways of bringing it to the attention of potential employers who will interview you. There are a number of strategies which you can use in addition to the traditional (and ineffective) method of posting a CV and covering letter to a targeted employer and waiting for a call to interview. These include, in ascending order of effectiveness, replying to advertisements, applying to employment/recruitment agencies, cold calling and networking. By using as many of these strategies as possible, without cutting any corners, you will greatly increase your chances of success.

Replying to Advertisements

While research has indicated that only about 15% of professional and managerial positions in Ireland are now advertised in the media, it would be very unwise to neglect this method for seeking employment. At least by monitoring the appointments pages in the national, provincial and local papers you will have a good sense of what opportunities are available, the skills that are being demanded and the salaries and wages applying in different areas of employment.

You should also check out *JobNews*, the weekly broadsheet which specialises in collating job advertisements for all categories of job seeker (and even allows you to place your own advertisement in the 'Situations Wanted' section free of charge.)

When you reply to an advertisement, be sure to read the details line by line, word by word, in order to know exactly what the needs of the potential employer are. Make a list of all the requirements specified and next to each write your relevant achievements. If your experience or qualifications don't match the advertisement exactly, use your skills and achievements creatively. Your achievements in themselves may generate enough interest to have you called to an interview — which is the object of the exercise in the first place.

Applying to Employment Agencies

Employment/recruitment agencies are usually the next most popular alternative considered by job seekers. These organisations are paid by employers to find suitable candidates for specific jobs. Over the last ten years, there has been a considerable increase in the number of such agencies offering their services throughout Ireland, no doubt reflecting their success rates in placing candidates in appropriate positions.

There are now agencies to cater for job needs ranging from entry level to management. Many specialise in particular fields such as accountancy, computers, engineering, insurance, nursing and secretarial work. Check which agencies are operating in your specific area of interest. The *Golden Pages* is an excellent source of information in this respect.

A note of caution, however. Employment agencies make money by placing people in jobs. They work for the employers, not for you. Therefore, unless you stick to your own agenda rather than that of the agency, you may find yourself attending interviews or even being offered positions which really are unsuitable.

Finally, once you have submitted your CV to the agencies which match your needs, forget about them and concentrate on the other methods of generating interviews. If they contact you regarding a position on their books, well and good. Otherwise, they have nothing to report, and you pestering them will do nothing to help your cause — and may even hinder it.

Cold Calling

This technique involves either telephoning on speculation or visiting without an appointment a number of potential employers. While such an approach requires great enthusiasm and assertiveness, there is no doubt that with proper practice and preparation, you stand a good chance of overcoming initial resistance and getting through to your target.

You should prepare a number of scripts in advance so that you will be totally at ease in introducing yourself and asking for a meeting. Be clear as to what exactly you want from such a discussion, whether it be to set up an interview directly or to establish referrals which can be followed up later. It is extremely important that you know as much as possible about who your potential employer is and what he or she does before you call. Remember, not alone is this a reflection of how you perform your work, it also enables you to identify what your potential employer's needs really are, and to focus on matching them with your achievements. By directing your conversation in a manner which makes people want to hear what you have to say, you will increase your chances of generating interviews.

If, on the other hand, you do not succeed in organising a meeting, you should still forward your CV with a covering letter, highlighting your most significant achievements and stating that you will be getting in contact again to arrange an appointment at a convenient time.

Networking

This is by far the most effective way of all to circulate your CV. Networking simply involves getting people to introduce or refer you to those who may have the opportunity to employ you, identify potential positions within the hidden job market for you or expand your list of contacts.

While there might not be a job opening when you first commence your discussion with a particular contact, you can always try to match your achievements to their perceived needs. At the best, and not beyond the realms of possibility, they might consider creating a job for you. Otherwise, you should concentrate on gaining further referrals to those who can in fact introduce you to the real opportunities in the hidden job market.

Almost every vacant position is discussed in some way with business colleagues or associates before it is advertised in the press or circulated to employment/recruitment agencies. Your task is to gain access to this information in advance of circulation and to present your profile and achievements before the vacancy is announced externally.

You should start your network by first contacting any friends whom you feel will respond favourably to your request to get together for a brief chat about your curriculum vitae. Develop this to include people whom you only know as acquaintances but who are very familiar with your target area. Finally, target your calls at those business contacts to whom you have been referred.

By adopting this approach, your first networking contacts will lead you to other business contacts who can get you started networking in your target area.

Meeting people from all professions such as accountants, solicitors, suppliers, distributors, trade associations, banks, customers, advertising agencies, public relations companies, estate agents, retired executives, etc., increases the opportunity of meeting somebody who can put you in contact with somebody else who knows of a specific need. Once inside the circle of information, you will have the advantage over other job seekers locked outside.

Remember, you are strongly advised to use a combination of all of the above strategies, to achieve results. Persevere. You'll be glad you did.

Chapter Eight

SAMPLE CVS

DENISE COLLINSON
65 Gower Street
London WC1E 6AH
071-387 8044

WORK EXPERIENCE:

1991 - Present   **FT SYSTEMS**   **London**

Project Manager

- Supervised 24 programming staff.
- Designed and implemented computerised time-sheet system, reducing administrative costs by 14% within 6 months.
- Established comprehensive in-house libraries of programmers' documentation and manuals.
- Developed warehouse and stock-taking systems for Sainsbury's and D.H. Evans.
- Wrote detailed specification for a computerised boning system used by British Meats.

1988 - 1991   **SYSTEMS SOFTWARE**   **Birmingham**

Project Manager

- Supervised 16 programming staff.
- Designed computerised system for Maternity Departments in 16 prestigious British hospitals.
- Developed computerised system for Casualty Departments, which was established as market leader in British, French and Belgian hospitals.
- Installed and provided support for more than 80 Novell networks in England and Wales.

EDUCATION:

1988   **LONDON UNIVERSITY**
Master of Business Administration

1987   **MANCHESTER UNIVERSITY**
Bachelor of Science (Honours)

BRENDAN O'DRISCOLL
Strokestown Road
Roscommon
(0903) 72418

LITIGATION

- Took instructions from clients, researched relevant case law and obtained Counsel's opinion on over 200 civil cases.

- Prepared briefs for court hearings, attended pre-court consultations and participated in pre-trial negotiations and settlements.

- Represented clients at hearings for debt collections, licensing applications and traffic violations.

PROBATE

- Obtained particulars of assets and liabilities, notified beneficiaries of entitlements and forwarded schedules to the Revenue Commissioners for assessment.

- Drafted and completed Capital Acquisitions Tax Returns, lodged proofs at Probate Office and discharged fees.

- Collected assets, paid debts and distributed balances of estates.

CONVEYANCING

- Drafted contracts, prepared deeds and investigated and perfected registered and unregistered titles in both Land Registry and the Registry of Deeds.

- Carried out planning investigations, drafted statutory declarations and closed sales.

- Purchased freeholds, prepared mortgage documentation and finalised clients' accounts.

WORK HISTORY:

1993 - 1994	Lynch, Abbott & Co., Castlerea Solicitor
1989 - 1993	Mary O'Brien & Co., Roscommon Apprentice Solicitor

EDUCATION:

1992	Incorporated Law Society Final Examination, Part III
1986	College of Commerce, Rathmines Diploma in Legal Studies
1985	University College Dublin BA (Honours)

GERALDINE MALONEY
24 Dublin Road
Portlaoise
Co. Laois
(0502) 53244

WORK EXPERIENCE

GALWAY REGIONAL HOSPITAL   1991 - 1994

Staff Nurse on 10-bedded Surgical Intensive Care Unit

- Cared for patients following coronary artery bypass surgery, neurosurgery, head injuries, multiple trauma, burns and multi-system failure.
- Responded to cardiac arrest calls throughout hospital.
- Set up and managed haemofiltration and ultrafiltration units.
- Counselled relatives of patients diagnosed as being 'brain dead'.

MATER PRIVATE HOSPITAL   1988 - 1991

Staff Nurse on 12-bedded Cardio-Thoracic Surgical Unit

- Prepared patients physically and psychologically for cardiac and thoracic surgery.
- Cared for and managed central venous lines, arterial lines, epidural catheters and chest drains.
- Interpreted E.C.G. on patients with cardiac monitor in situ.

ROYAL CITY OF DUBLIN HOSPITAL   1985 - 1988

Student Nurse

- Provided patient care pre and post major and minor surgery

EDUCATION

ROYAL COLLEGE OF SURGEONS, DUBLIN   1992
Diploma in Nursing Management

ROYAL CITY OF DUBLIN HOSPITAL   1988
State Registered Nurse

SEAMUS BOLAND
26 The Close
Gorey
Co. Wexford
(053) 25685

JOB TARGET: MECHANICAL ENGINEER

ABILITIES:

- Solve mechanical problems using engineering theory and practical experience.
- Supervise engineering workshop personnel.
- Inspect machine components for defects, fatigue, wear.
- Program CNC machinery, CMM, Robots.
- Trouble shoot on mechanical machinery.
- Use CAD/CAM systems and general machine shop equipment.
- Program computers in C, Fortran, COBOL and Basic.

ACHIEVEMENTS:

- Manufactured test equipment for refrigeration systems. Overhauled, maintained and inspected diesel electric locomotives, electro-motive units (DART), refrigeration and air-conditioning systems.
- Supervised 16 engineering personnel.
- Designed and manufactured returnable crates and jigs for shipping department.
- Assessed production line space requirements and arrangements.
- Tested adhesive versus spotwelding on paint/cake components.

WORK EXPERIENCE:

1991 - 1994	Thermo King Europe, Dublin Manufacturing Engineer
1990 - 1991	Irish Rail Mechanical Engineer

EDUCATION:

1990	College of Technology, Bolton Street BSc in Manufacturing Engineering

ANNETTE FARRELL
67 Patrick Street
Cork
(021) 363456

PROPERTY MANAGEMENT:

- Managed 24 private accommodation properties in Cork city and suburbs.
- Advertised vacancies in daily and weekly newspapers.
- Interviewed potential tenants, selected those suitable and initiated letting agreements.
- Collected rents on a weekly basis, ensured payphones were operational and dealt with any problems.
- Maintained and tended to gardens and other common areas.
- Recorded all transactions related to the properties.

SYSTEMS DEVELOPMENT:

- Computerised sales and purchases accounting functions, reducing administration cost by £8,000 per annum.
- Tested software and identified systems errors.
- Monitored the progress of 'dummy' invoices through the system, ascertaining that relevant balances were updated.

ADMINISTRATION:

- Coded and prepared over 100 invoices and credit notes on a daily basis for data entry.
- Inputted invoice details to Phillips Novell Sky mainframe system.
- Provided price quotations to customers in response to telephone enquiries.
- Supervised 3 clerical assistants.

WORK HISTORY:

1991 - 1994	Bandon Properties Ltd., Cork Property Manager
1987 - 1991	Thompson Plumbing Supplies, Mallow Office Manager
1985 - 1987	McDonagh & Sons, Skibbereen Bookkeeper

EDUCATION:

1985	Cork RTC Diploma in Business Studies

SIOBHAN RYAN
8 Halston Street
Dublin 7
(01) 8733138

WORK EXPERIENCE:

LIFFEY STATIONERY SUPPLIES   **1990 - Present**
Dublin

Office Administrator

- Managed all printing operations, including both thermo and flat print on compliment slips, letterheads and invoices.
- Co-ordinated despatch drivers, organising all paperwork to enable them to make deliveries efficiently.
- Controlled the computer invoicing system, ensuring all invoices were processed correctly and credit notes were issued for goods returned.
- Arranged appointments and dealt with all customer queries.

MURPHY'S OFFICE SUPPLIES   **1987 - 1990**
Cork

Buyer (1988 - 1990)

- Represented company at stationery and equipment shows, liaising with new suppliers and negotiating terms and conditions of contract.
- Ordered all stocks and one-off purchases, receiving goods when delivered and checking to ensure they matched delivery notes.
- Met with company representatives to discuss new lines and negotiate discounts.
- Checked stocks on a regular basis, maintaining balances at a minimum level.

Office Junior (1987 - 1988)

- Processed orders from customers via telephone and fax, product coding each to facilitate efficient ordering from suppliers.
- Prepared those emergency orders which needed to be delivered within 3 hours.
- Filed suppliers' dispatch notes an1 customers' orders and delivery notes.
- Typed all company correspondence and tenders.

EDUCATION:

1986   SCOIL ÍDE, FINGLAS
              Executive Secretarial Course

SEAN O'ROURKE
25 Dalysfort Road
Salthill
Galway
(091) 621169

ACCOUNTING:

- Wrote up books of first entry and posted balances to ledger accounts on a daily basis.
- Maintained monthly debtors and creditors control accounts.
- Operated cheque receipts and cheque payments books.
- Prepared monthly bank reconciliation statements and queried discrepancies with the bank.
- Recorded VAT movements and filed VAT returns on a bi-monthly basis.

CUSTOMER SERVICES:

- Provided professional support service to customers, ensuring timely deliveries and quality service.
- Compiled and presented a status report of customer queries and follow-up action taken.
- Relayed product information to potential and existing customers.
- Conversed with customers in English, French, German, Italian and Russian.

SALES:

- Developed selling programmes offering company products and services to existing and potential customers.
- Compiled monthly analysis of sales by product, region and sales representative.
- Maintained and serviced existing accounts.

EMPLOYMENT HISTORY:

1989 - 1994	Galway Crystal Customer Services Officer
1985 - 1989	Corrib Gas Ltd. Sales Representative
1984 - 1985	Salthill Linen Company Bookkeeper

EDUCATION:

| 1984 | Leaving Certificate — 4 Honours |

YVONNE CLANCY
2 Main Street
Drogheda
Co. Louth
(041) 52356

JOB TARGET: QUANTITY SURVEYOR

ABILITIES:

- Prepare cost plans, interim valuations and final accounts.
- Measure buildings and civil engineering works.
- Produce drawings and specifications.
- Build up rates and prepare estimates.
- Source, obtain, assimilate and present information effectively.
- Use ELSIE and CATO software.
- Work under pressure and to tight deadlines.

ACHIEVEMENTS:

- Prepared Bills of Quantities for 4 shopping centres in Dublin, Limerick, Cork and Galway.
- Drafted cost estimates for schools, libraries and rest homes.
- Produced specifications for 104 houses built as part of Dublin Inner City Development Scheme.
- Prepared cost estimates for extension of Gresham Hotel, totalling in excess of £850,000.
- Supervised staff of 5 estimators.

WORK HISTORY:

1989 - Present   DUBLIN COUNTY COUNCIL
                    Quantity Surveyor

1985 - 1989   THOMPSON, O'NEILL & ASSOCIATES, DUBLIN
                    Estimator

EDUCATION:

1993   TRINITY COLLEGE DUBLIN
            B.Sc. (Surveying) — 2:1 Honours

1990   BOLTON STREET COLLEGE OF TECHNOLOGY
            Diploma in Construction Economics

JOHN MURPHY
21 Limerick Road
Nenagh
Co. Tipperary
(062) 62649

WORK EXPERIENCE:

BANK OF IRELAND   1970 - 1994
Nenagh

Manager (1985)
Assistant Manager (1983)
Officer (1979)
Senior Bank Official (1974)

- Assisted private and corporate loan applications for amounts up to £250,000, reviewing loans granted, monitoring ongoing performance and tracking adherence with original agreements.

- Prepared branch budgets ranging from £750,000 - £15m. over a three year period, rectifying deviations as appropriate and assessing final outcomes.

- Identified, researched and implemented a change in the branch fee structure, resulting in an increase in profits of £75,000 per annum.

- Liaised with all foreign exchange clients, advising on alternative strategies and identifying the most cost-effective and appropriate methods of shipment and payment.

- Co-ordinated the computerisation of a branch accounting system catering for 45 staff over a 9-month period, ensuring the accurate transfer, verification and updating of all financial data.

- Trained teams of 10-12 staff members in product development, quality service and profitability awareness, thereby improving efficiency and effectiveness.

EDUCATION:

1980   UNIVERSITY COLLEGE DUBLIN
            B. Comm. Degree (First Class Honours)

1974   INSTITUTE OF BANKERS IN IRELAND
            Banking Certificate

CLAIRE QUINN
'Inishowen'
Iona Road
Glasnevin
Dublin 9
(01) 8307240

WORK EXPERIENCE:

Summer 1993	Clifden Hotel Waitress
	DPS Electronics Secretary
Summer 1992	Brooking PR Public Relations Assistant
Summer 1990/91	Caesar's Leisure and Entertainment Centre Cashier

SPORTS:

- Participated in and reached final of Dominican Basketball League 4 times.
- Secretary of Basketball team in Fifth Year and Captain in Sixth Year.
- Represented school at Swimming, Athletics, Cross-Country and Tennis.

DEBATING:

- Participated in competitive and friendly debates against other schools.

MUSIC AND DRAMA:

- Member of Dublin Secondary Schoolgirl's Choir and Dominican College Sixth Year Choir.
- Attended Gaiety School of Acting for several years.
- Acted in *Romeo and Juliet*, St Patrick's College, Drumcondra (1989) and *The Merchant of Venice*, Presentation Convent (1992).

EDUCATION:

1988 - 1993   Dominican Convent, 24 Eccles St, Dublin 1
                Leaving Certificate - 6 Honours

JOHN BRADLEY
67 O'Malley Park
Enniscorthy
Co Wexford
(053) 247532

JOB TARGET: WAITER/CATERING ASSISTANT

ABILITIES:

- Provide à la carte and table d'hôte style service.
- Set tables for up to eight-course meals.
- Receive and seat customers.
- Take orders from customers and liaise with the kitchen.
- Serve wine and other beverages.
- Perform silver service and French style food service.
- Handle customer enquiries and complaints efficiently.
- Clear tables systematically.

ACHIEVEMENTS:

- Catered for all types and sizes of functions in a wide range of establishments.
- Performed French style food service for up to 60 people.
- Provided room service in a 5 star de luxe castle hotel.
- Served in dining room, providing breakfasts, lunches and dinners to 400 people daily.

EMPLOYMENT HISTORY:

1992 - to date	The Great Wall Restaurant, Gorey *Waiter*
1990 - 1992	The Gresham Hotel, Dublin *Waiter*
1988 - 1990	Dromoland Castle Hotel, Co Clare *Waiter*

EDUCATION

1988	CBS Enniscorthy Leaving Certificate — 2 honours, 5 passes

DEBBIE MORAN
52 Dorset Street, Dublin 1
(01) 6745908

WORK EXPERIENCE

SCHOOLS AND COLLEGES THEATRE COMPANY   **1991-1994**
A fringe company specialising in promoting theatre in over 800 secondary schools nationally and employing 25-30 actors on an ongoing basis.
Administrative Assistant

- Targeted, promoted and arranged suitable venues for over 400 performances in 28 counties.

- Notified actors, arranged transport and co-ordinated travel and accommodation arrangements for the entire cast.

- Established pricing structures, invoiced schools, distributed payments and maintained records of each event.

- Developed a comprehensive directory of post-primary schools nationwide, which enhanced the efficiency and effectiveness of the promotional function.

- Designed logos and layout for company stationery, flyers and other publicity material.

- Arranged auditions, collected fees, organised facilities and maintained a library for 160 students attending the part-time Diploma in Acting and Stage Management at the Dorset School of Acting.

HOWTH HERITAGE SOCIETY   **1990-1991**
A centre promoting interest in the history of the hinterland of Howth and facilitating the research of genealogical information by members of the public.
Researcher

- Computerised register of 150,000 pre-1900 births, deaths and marriages of 6 local parishes.

- Promoted the sale of local history booklets, *Past Imperfect?* and *St Anne's Church* in 56 outlets.

- Researched and wrote a booklet on mediaeval castles in the Howth area.

HODGES FIGGIS   **1989-1990**
Largest city centre bookstore, catering for comprehensive range of customers and with a turnover in excess of 80,000 titles per year.
Sales Assistant

- Advised customers on choice of titles, organised stocking of Irish and English literature sections, arranged displays of best selling volumes.

EDUCATION:

ST PATRICK'S COLLEGE, MAYNOOTH   **1990-**
Master of Arts (Part-time)

ST PATRICK'S COLLEGE, MAYNOOTH   **1986-1989**
Bachelor of Arts (English, History and Anthropology)

JOHN MOLLOY
22 Tramore Road
Waterford
(051) 367943

WORK EXPERIENCE

BAUSCH & LOMB IRELAND   1989 - Present
Waterford   (Manufacture of contact lens - 1,000 employees)

Senior Personnel Officer (Direct report to Human Resources/Quality Director)

- Developed, introduced and trained 400 employees on a new Performance Management System.

- Managed the successful introduction of 3-cycle shift process within the lens manufacturing facility.

- Led a Quality Improvement team to evaluate and improve the comany newsletter. This resulted in a quality publication which is now produced in-house.

- Introduced the Long Service Award Programme, which to date has recognised 300 employees for between 10 and 25 years service at numerous lunches and dinners held over the last 5 years.

- Developed 40 human resource policies and procedures for the Irish operation.

- Managed the introduction of a flexitime system which led to a major improvement in the attendance recording process.

ERGO COMPUTER (IRELAND) LIMITED   1985 - 1989
Dublin   (Manufacture of mainframe computers - 500 employees)

Senior Personnel Officer   (Direct report to Human Resources Director)

- Played a key role in setting up and managing the Outplacement Service as part of the redundancy programme, which included giving advice on curriculum vitae preparation, interview techniques, taxation, pensions and counselling employees.

- Received an Excellence Award for my role in the redundancy programme.

- Prepared Ireland's annual salary plan for submission to Ergo Corporation for approval.

- Introduced and implemented a computerised personnel system to ensure on-line availability of data concerning personnel issues. Received an Excellence Award for my achievements in this project.

- Represented Ergo Computers on the FIE Equality Network to promote the concept of equality in the workplace.

EDUCATION

National Diploma in Personnel Management (Distinction)   **1988**
Bachelor of Commerce (2.1)   **1984**

JANE O'BRIEN
66 Orwell Park
Ballinasloe
Co Galway
(091) 769543

BAR WORK

- Served customers in a range of public houses and nightclubs.
- Stocked shelves and carried out regular stocktaking functions.
- Performed nightly count of tills and reconciled differences.

WAITRESSING

- Served in a carvery, providing breakfasts, lunches, dinners and suppers for 400-500 customers daily.
- Provided supper service in city centre nightclub for over 100 customers.
- Dispensed 50-100 evening meals to customers in a cabaret lounge.

SALES ASSISTANT

- Served and assisted customers in a London department store.
- Performed cashier duties, including balancing of tills.
- Ordered stocks using computerised inventory system.
- Set up in-store fixture displays.

CLOAKROOM ATTENDANT

- Designed and operated a system to receive and return garments and bags for busy Galway nightclub.
- Controlled movements of cash and balanced tills nightly.

EMPLOYMENT HISTORY

1991 - to date	CJ's Nightclub, Galway Bar Person/Cloakroom Attendant
1990 - 1991	The Stroll Inn, Salthill, Galway Bar Person/Waitress
1989 - 1990	DH Evans, London Sales Assistant
	Shakespeare's Head, London Bar Person

EDUCATION

1993	Institute of Accounting Technicians in Ireland: Foundation Level
1989	Leaving Certificate — 4 honours

CATHAL COURTNEY
7 St Alphonsus Road
Dundalk
Co Louth
(042) 815166

JOB TARGET: BANK OFFICIAL

CAPABILITIES

- Set up new accounts, completing relevant documentation and promoting ancillary services.

- Input data into mainframe computer system and produce hard copy.

- Perform cashiering duties, handling lodgements, withdrawals and foreign exchange transactions.

- Deal professionally and calmly with customers' queries and complaints.

- Handle all routine and administrative work such as maintaining records, tracing information and co-ordinating office services.

- Handle high pressure situations and deadlines.

- Compose and prepare routine correspondence.

- Analyse data into relevant financial statistics.

- Prepare financial and other reports.

ACHIEVEMENTS

- Set up 40-50 new accounts daily for client companies seeking factoring facilities.

- Prepared source documents of debtor information, which specified personal details, credit limits and terms of credit.

- Keyboarded data from completed documents into IBM mainframe system and produced a hard copy of information.

- Recorded payments received from debtors, reconciled ledgers and brought outstanding accounts to the attention of superiors.

- Collated account details of debtors entering liquidation and returned these to client companies.

- Traded in stocks and shares in Irish public companies, which included Golden Vale, Irish Life and Bula Resources Holding.

WORK HISTORY

1990-1991 **ULSTER BANK INTERNATIONAL FACTORS**
Clerical Assistant (work experience programme)

EDUCATION

1993 **PORTOBELLO COLLEGE**
Diploma in Financial Services (with Credit)

JANET O'KEEFFE
7 Main Street
Drumshanbo, Co Leitrim
(078) 550864
JOB TARGET: SECRETARY/OFFICE ADMINISTRATOR

ABILITIES

- Touch type at 50 wpm.
- Use WordPerfect 5.1, WordStar 2000, Database 5 software packages.
- Operate fax machines, photocopiers and franking machines.
- Compose correspondence to clients/customers.
- Manage a computerised stock control system.
- Process invoices, cheques and credit/debit notes manually and on computer.
- Prepare control accounts and bank reconciliation statements.

ACHIEVEMENTS

- Typed reports, correspondence and labels on IBM compatible computers and typewriters.
- Operated a 30-line switchboard.
- Used the Jarman computerised stock control system and analysed stock movements between branches.
- Inputted invoices, credit/debit notes and payments/receipts to computerised accounting systems.
- Wrote up cheque receipts and cheque payments books.
- Prepared monthly bank reconciliation statements and queried discrepancies with the bank where necessary.
- Maintained creditors control accounts.
- Organised bank deposits (including Visa and American Express), disbursing and balancing petty cash.

WORK HISTORY

1990 - to date	Various temporary and administrative positions, including assignments with Nitrigin Eireann Teoranta, DTI Systems Ltd, Preston Services Ltd, Homecare Furniture Ltd, and Carney Cleardrains Ltd
1988 - 1990	O'Hanlon's Gift Shop, Carrick-on-Shannon Full-time Secretary/Receptionist

EDUCATION

1988	Littledales Secretarial College	Commercial Course
1987	Presentation Convent Drumshanbo	Leaving Certificate

GRÁINNE REILLY
Dublin Road
Naas
Co Kildare
(045) 533452

ACCOUNTING

- Wrote up books of prime entry and posted balances to ledger accounts on a daily basis.
- Maintained monthly debtor and creditors control accounts.
- Operated cheque receipts and cheque payments books.
- Prepared monthly bank reconciliation statements and queried discrepancies with the bank.
- Recorded VAT movements and filed VAT returns on a bi-monthly basis.

ORGANISATION

- Set up basic accounting system for small publishing company.
- Founded College soccer team and entered it into ITCFA League.
- Collected subscriptions and performed public relations activities on behalf of the soccer team.
- Organised outings and social events on behalf of the College Student Union.

REPRESENTATION

- Co-ordinated activities of the Student Union, ensure communication was maintained between students and representatives.
- Liaised with College staff and lecturers on behalf of students experiencing difficulties.
- Promoted College at presentations and Open Days.

WORK EXPERIENCE

1991 - 1993 (Summers)   Black Tower Publishing, Naas, Co Kildare
Accounts Clerk

1989 - 1991 (Summers)   Ryan's Filling Station
Petrol Attendant

EDUCATION

1991 - 1994   Association of Accounting Technicians
Portobello College, Dublin

ANNE BARRY
25, The Drive
Castlebar, Co Mayo
(098) 723646
JOB TARGET: FINANCIAL ACCOUNTANT

ABILITIES

- Supervise accounting staff through all phases of computerised accounting system through trial balance and issuance of financial statements.
- Develop, analyse and report monthly forecasts of net sales, operating expenses and capital spending.
- Co-ordinate and prepare annual operating and capital budgets.
- Issue financial reports to substantiate line of credit on a monthly basis.
- Co-ordinate all phases of financial recording through monthly financial statements.
- Prepare change in balance sheet analysis, cash flow and expense variance analysis.
- Direct operation management in cost reduction/containment actions to meet budget objectives.
- Manage cheque and cash disbursement system, co-ordinate system changes and updates, and maintain internal controls.
- Analyse and budget staffing needs.
- Recruit candidates and conduct performance reviews.

ACHIEVEMENTS

- Prepared, processed and updated journal entries for monthly management accounts, within 3 days of end of period.
- Completed monthly profit and loss account, balance sheet and notes to the accounts using Lotus 1-2-3, within 2 days of producing management accounts.
- Briefed financial controller on order processing and customer status under upgrade program for weekly meetings.
- Approved invoices and credit notes weekly, prepared daily shipments reports and reconciled revenue per sales ledger to shipment records.
- Completed monthly bank reconciliation on payroll and current accounts, implemented internal controls on issuance of cheques and advised financial accountant regarding significant movements on the account.
- Prepared standard and scrap expense variance analysis reports for monthly management meetings.

WORK HISTORY

AT&T NETWORK SYSTEMS IRELAND   **1990-**
Manufacturer of telecommunications products: annual turnover £25m approx
Assistant Accountant

EDUCATION

Griffith College, Dublin   **1992**
CIMA
Dublin City University   **1990**
BA IN ACCOUNTANCY AND FINANCE (HONS)

BRENDAN RYAN
23 Laurel Avenue
Greystones, Co Wicklow
(01) 8763456

JOB TARGET: MAINTENANCE FITTER/TURNER

ABILITIES

- Overhaul, maintain and inspect machine components for defects, fatigue, wear.
- Manufacture fixtures, stands and tools using MIG, stick and gas welding.
- Use general machine shop equipment, eg lathe, milling machine, radial drill, cylindrical grinder and hand/power tools.
- Program CMM, CNC Machinery, Robots.
- Perform industrial plumbing work for air, gas and water.
- Maintain records of all work performed.
- Train apprentices to build modules.

ACHIEVEMENTS

- Built paint shop for aircraft engine cases, which involved installing a water extraction unit, manufacturing fixtures, inserting heaters, and carrying out pipework for breathing apparatus, spray gun and gas heaters.
- Drained and disassembled chrome, nickel, silver, wax, cyanide and water tanks in plating shop, removed pipework and redirected feed, and facilitated installation of replacement tanks.
- Erected scaffolding, dismantled and reassembled 2-section, 15 foot steel and glass partitions and manufactured stands for pneumatic systems in the fuel shop.
- Dismantled heaters and diverted 25′ main steam line from boiler house to facilitate movement of cranes.
- Assembled and installed components and sub-assemblies for aircraft engines.

WORK HISTORY

1985 - to date	AERIRELAND LTD
	Blessington, Co Wicklow
	Fitter/Turner

EDUCATION

1988	Jet Engines and their Overhaul Procedures Certificate
	Bolton Street College of Technology
1987	Mechanical Engineering Technician Certificate (Part 1 and 2)
	City & Guilds
1986	Mechanical Trade Certificate (Junior and Senior)
	Department of Education

PERSONAL RECORD

NOTES

NOTES

NOTES

NOTES

Don't miss

The Original
WOLFHOUND GUIDE TO EVENING CLASSES
and Leisure Learning in Dublin City and County

° Now in its 20th edition

° Covers a full range of adult education activities

° Sports, clubs, associations, meetings

° Hundreds of activities from archery to yachting

° Over 4,000 entries

° Many free courses, and others for as little as £3!

Packed with great ways to fill those winter evenings
— career-oriented courses, languages, personal
development, sports, crafts, adventure, music,
business, creative writing, art, computers

Still only £1.99

Available from Dublin booksellers or from
WOLFHOUND PRESS
68 Mountjoy Square, Dublin 1. Tel 01 8740354
Call or write for our catalogue.

The Original Mercier

GUIDE TO EVENING CLASSES
in Cork City and County

Complete and detailed guide to over 1,000 courses in public and private centres throughout Cork city and county. Published by Mercier Press in association with Wolfhound Press, this comprehensive and reliable guide lists venues and prices for classes, clubs, sports and activities to keep you busy all year round.

° Daytime and evening courses

° Home Study

° Adult Education

° Sport

° Leisure

Don't miss your copy!

JOB HUNTING?

CHANGING CAREERS?

FACING REDUNDANCY?

COMING UP FOR APPRAISAL OR PROMOTION?

THINKING ABOUT SELF-EMPLOYMENT?

IN THE WRONG JOB?

NO CAREER PLAN?

To make an appointment, or for information on the comprehensive range of professional guidance services offered, phone or call to:

Áine Keenan,
THE CAREER DOCTOR,
Suite 6, 24/26 Dame St., Dublin 2
Tel.: 6795133 Fax.: 6770510